YoungWriters

My First Acrostic

Derbyshire & Nottinghamshire

Edited by Allison Jones

First published in Great Britain in 2010 by:

Young Writers

Young Writers
Remus House
Coltsfoot Drive
Peterborough
PE2 9JX
Telephone: 01733 890066
Website: www.youngwriters.co.uk

SB ISBN 978-1-84924-859-4

Foreword

The 'My First Acrostic' collection was developed by Young Writers specifically for Key Stage 1 children. The poetic form is simple, fun and gives the young poet a guideline to shape their ideas, yet at the same time leaves room for their imagination and creativity to begin to blossom.

Due to the young age of the entrants we have enjoyed rewarding their effort by including as many of the poems as possible. Our hope is that seeing their work in print will encourage the children to grow and develop their writing skills to become our poets of tomorrow.

Young Writers has been publishing children's poetry for over 19 years. Our aim is to nurture creativity in our children and young adults, to give them an interest in poetry and an outlet to express themselves. This latest collection will act as a milestone for the young poets and one that will be enjoyable to revisit again and again.

Contents

The Poems

Me

B est friends with Owen.
R ick is a boy.
A lways a great friend.
D ylan is my friend.
L ike to play with Owen.
E xcellent to my friends.
Y ear 2 is my class.

Bradley Johnson (6)
Abercrombie Primary School, Chesterfield

Me

G reat and pretty.
E xcellent at work.
O lives I do not like.
R eally, really pretty.
G reat at running.
I am good for my teacher.
A m sensible and helpful.

Georgia Jolley (6)
Abercrombie Primary School, Chesterfield

Me

K icks a ball.
A imee Is my friend.
T he friend I play with is Ben.
Y ou are my best friend Ebony.

Katy Webster (6)
Abercrombie Primary School, Chesterfield

Me

Always playing.
Makes models.
Everyone's friend.
Like to play with my friends.
Is always kind.
Always help my mum.

Amelia Adams (7)
Abercrombie Primary School, Chesterfield

Me

Always nice and kind.
Likes to work.
Extra good in class.
Says nice things.
Helps other people.
Always an angel.

Alesha White (6)
Abercrombie Primary School, Chesterfield

Me

Tafara is my friend.
Helps people.
Owen is my friend.
Makes things.
Always plays nicely.
Says nice things.

Thomas Simcoe (6)
Abercrombie Primary School, Chesterfield

Me

Excellent at writing.
Be a nice girl.
Owen is my friend.
Nice girl to others.
You are a nice friend Aleisha.

Ebony Schofield (6)
Abercrombie Primary School, Chesterfield

Me

Always a great friend.
Is cool.
Makes people laugh.
Excellent at waiting.
Extremely good girl.

Aimee Fox (6)
Abercrombie Primary School, Chesterfield

Me

Careful, kind and helpful.
On the way home I play.
Really a great friend.
You are great Kyle.

Cory Turner (6)
Abercrombie Primary School, Chesterfield

Me

J ump over the stairs.
A lways wears hats.
C akes are yummy.
K indness.

Jack Jolley (6)
Abercrombie Primary School, Chesterfield

Chips

C runchy
H ot
I ncredible
P otatoey
S aucy.

Daniel Fleckney (5)
Ashbrook Infant School, Borrowash

Beans

B rilliant
E xtreme
A mazing
N ice
S upper.

Daniel O'Sullivan (7)
Ashbrook Infant School, Borrowash

Strawberries

S oft
T asty
R ed
A mazing flavour
W onderful
B eautiful
E njoy with your pudding
R eally good with cream
R eally nice
I ce cream
E at them
S quishy.

Tia Thornley (6)
Ashbrook Infant School, Borrowash

Fishfingers

F loppy
I have them with tomato Ketchup
S oft
H ot in the oven
F at
I have them all the time at McDonald's
N ice
G olden
E at them with chips and beans
R ising
S limy.

Rebecca Winrow (7)
Ashbrook Infant School, Borrowash

Ice Lollies

I love it
Creamy cream
Extremely nice

Lemoney
Oh so yummy
Lovely
Limey
Icy
Excellent
Slippy.

Dominic Calcutt (5)
Ashbrook Infant School, Borrowash

Strawberry

Surprise
Tasty
Rosy
Amazing
Wet
Brilliant
Excellent
Red
Round
Yummy.

Sophie Jones (6)
Ashbrook Infant School, Borrowash

Pork Chops

P ink
O pen your mouth
R eally tasty
K eep it

C an we have them every day?
H ot
O h my goodness it is delicious
P ops
S crumptious.

Joe Jackson (7)
Ashbrook Infant School, Borrowash

Chocolate

C runchy
H ot
O ops
C hunky
O k I'll have chocolate
L ovely
A mazing
T ight
E xstreme.

Isaac Sherlock Hewkin (6)
Ashbrook Infant School, Borrowash

Lollipops

Lovely lollipops
Oh so lovely on a hot day
Lemon lollipops
Lickable lollipops
I think they're yummy
Penguin
Orange
Pleasant
Surprising.

Georgia Reynolds (5)
Ashbrook Infant School, Borrowash

Chocolate

Crunchy
Hot
Only a little bit
Cold
Orange flavour
Lovely
Amazing
Tasty
Eat it for your pudding.

Joshua Woolley (6)
Ashbrook Infant School, Borrowash

Spaghetti

S limy, slippery, squelchy
P erfect
A bit damp
G olden
H ot
E ating
T ry it
T asty
I love it!

James Astle (6)
Ashbrook Infant School, Borrowash

Chocolate

C hocolate
H ot and warming
O range
C hunky
O h yum-yum
L emony
A box for Mummy
T asty
E xtremely exciting.

Louis Barton (5)
Ashbrook Infant School, Borrowash

Bubblegum

B ang
U gly
B urst
B oom
L ong
E verlasting
G reen
U p your nose
M outh chews.

Tommi Swarbrook (6)
Ashbrook Infant School, Borrowash

Spaghetti

S lippery
P eppers
A ppley
G arlic bread
H ot
E ggy
T omatoey
T oo nice
I t goes everywhere.

Chelsea Smith (6)
Ashbrook Infant School, Borrowash

Ice Cream

I like
C hocolate
E normous

C reamy ice cream
R aspberry
E at with a little spoon
A pple
M elting.

Madison Wood (5)
Ashbrook Infant School, Borrowash

Apple Pie

A mazing
P urple
P inky
L ovely
E ggy

P lease don't eat it all!
I like it
E njoyable.

Ruby Miall (6)
Ashbrook Infant School, Borrowash

Ice cream

I like strawberry
C old
E ager to eat

C ream
R eally cold
E xciting flavours
A mazing
M elt.

Kieron Eyre (5)
Ashbrook Infant School, Borrowash

Pancakes

P erfect
A stounding
N ew
C rispy
A mazing
K ind
E ver so tasty
S yrupy.

Sam O'Sullivan (7)
Ashbrook Infant School, Borrowash

Tomatoes

Twizzle
Orange
Munching
Amazing
Tomato
Open the bottle
Excellent!
Sauce.

Laura Monk (5)
Ashbrook Infant School, Borrowash

Sausages

Sizzling
Amazing
Use them to eat
Sausage
And mash
Greasy
Eat them for tea
Sooty.

George Casartelli (5)
Ashbrook Infant School, Borrowash

T asty
A ppley
R unny
D elicious.

Joshua Hardy (6)
Ashbrook Infant School, Borrowash

Nutella

N utty
U nlikely to resist it
T asty
E xceptional on bread
L ots of chocolate
L ovely
A trocious on sausages!

Henry Saunders (6)
Ashbrook Infant School, Borrowash

Chicken

Crispy
Happy
In the oven
Cook it
Keep it
Enjoy
Nuggets.

Benjamin Tipping (5)
Ashbrook Infant School, Borrowash

Sausages

Sizzle
Apple and pork
Under the grill
Supper
Amazing
Great
Eat them up.

Kate Stott (6)
Ashbrook Infant School, Borrowash

Banana

Brilliant and yummy
Are enormous and delicious
Never try sweets too sweet
Amazing crescent
Nice and healthy
Always love them.

Maya Beadsmoore (6)
Ashbrook Infant School, Borrowash

Sweets

Sugary
We like to
Eat a lot
Everyone loves them
Tasty
Sweet.

Marcus Brown (5)
Ashbrook Infant School, Borrowash

Banana

Big
Astounding
Nice
And it is yummy
New
Amazing.

Emily Ward (5)
Ashbrook Infant School, Borrowash

Banana

B riliant
A milkshake flavour
N ice
A s tasty as pie
N ice in my tummy
A box for Mum.

Erin Blaney (6)
Ashbrook Infant School, Borrowash

Cookie

C runchy and sugary,
O h so yummy,
'O nly one more,' says Mum,
K itty is the greedy one
I t makes you want *more!*
'E xcellent!' I say.

Daisy Sheppard (7)
Ashbrook Infant School, Borrowash

Burger

B eef
U gly
R aining
G ood
E at
R ound.

Lewis Tipping (7)
Ashbrook Infant School, Borrowash

ets

ur
Wicked
Exciting colours
Eat slowly
Toffee
Smelly.

Amélie Culley (5)
Ashbrook Infant School, Borrowash

Dinner

Doughnuts
I like them
Not for dinner though!
Nice
Eat it up
Ready for pudding.

Olivia Zarza Fox (5)
Ashbrook Infant School, Borrowash

Apples

Amazing they taste,
Pretty good apples,
Precious to me,
Likeable I think,
Excellent,
Short not long.

Erin Hughes (7)
Ashbrook Infant School, Borrowash

Orange

Orange
Rolly
Amazing
Nobbly
Golden
Everyone likes them.

Abigail Burr (6)
Ashbrook Infant School, Borrowash

Banana

Bumpy
And
New
Amazing
Nice
And yummy.

Connor Brooke (6)
Ashbrook Infant School, Borrowash

Chips

Crunchy
Hot
Irresistible
Perfect
Supper.

Laura Mann (7)
Ashbrook Infant School, Borrowash

Jelly

J ubbly
E very day
L ovely
L ava
Y ou can taste it!

Kirsten Abbott (5)
Ashbrook Infant School, Borrowash

Jelly

J ubbly
E ver so lovely
L ovely
L ove it
Y ummy!

Bradley Beeston (6)
Ashbrook Infant School, Borrowash

Beans

B rill
E xtreme
A stounding
N ice
S ticky.

Aiden Gall (6)
Ashbrook Infant School, Borrowash

Jelly

J ammy
E xciting
L ovely
L emony
Y ummy!

Lauren Gall (5)
Ashbrook Infant School, Borrowash

Jelly

J uicy, gooey and slimy,
E xcited, shiny and red,
L ovely strawberry-flavoured,
L oveable, nice and yummy,
Y ummy scrumptious jelly.

Lydia Hill (7)
Ashbrook Infant School, Borrowash

Juicy

J uicy
E at
L ovely
L ime
Y um.

Deacon Cartlidge (6)
Ashbrook Infant School, Borrowash

Jelly

Jelly wobbles
Empty jelly
Lumpy jelly
Lovely jelly
Yellow jelly.

Louie Williams (6)
Ashbrook Infant School, Borrowash

Jelly

Juicy
Extreme
Lovely
Lemony
Yummy.

Ben Cuttriss (6)
Ashbrook Infant School, Borrowash

Chips

Crinkly
Hot
I love them
Plateful
Salad.

Abbie Pamplin (6)
Ashbrook Infant School, Borrowash

Chips

C runchy
H ot
I n the oven
P ointed
S alty.

Jackson Wood (7)
Ashbrook Infant School, Borrowash

Pizza

P erfect
I n the oven.
Z ingy
Z izzly
A mazing.

Jenna Delbridge (5)
Ashbrook Infant School, Borrowash

Apple

A mazing juicy apple
P umpkin-shaped apples
P eeling apples
L ovely apple
E xciting.

Callum Woolley (6)
Ashbrook Infant School, Borrowash

Fish And Chips

Fishy
I buy it
Salty
Huge

Amazing
Nice and greasy
Delicious

Crunchy
Hot
I love them
Peas go with it
Soft.

Billy Beal (6)
Ashbrook Infant School, Borrowash

Strawberry

Soft
Tasty
Rosy
Ashamed
Wet
Berry
Eggy
Red
Runny
Yummy.

Rosie Cox (6)
Ashbrook Infant School, Borrowash

Theo Francis

Theo is strong and kind and
Happy all the time because he has good friends.
Eats cakes and chocolates and
Oranges and dreams of going to the moon.

Firefighter Francis - it's me!
Running is my favourite thing because it's exercise.
Apples and bananas are healthy foods.
Nice time at the park playing with my little sister.
Cricket and football after school keep me fit.
Ice cream is tasty and everyone eats it on a hot day.
School is cool because it's tidy and we learn about Jesus and God and dolphins and houses, and we write and colour and dance and we learn not to trap our fingers in the door!

Theo Francis (5)
Awsworth Primary School, Awsworth

Me, My Cousin And My Sister

I am India, the one you'll love best.
Next I love my friends and family because they are the best.
Dogs are my favourite animal, but I don't have one.
I like playing with my cousin and my sister.
Awsworth Primary School is the best school in the world.

India Snaith (6)
Awsworth Primary School, Awsworth

All About Buddy

My pet dog Buddy
You would think he's very funny

Parks and woods, you'd find him there
Every day everywhere
Tickles and cuddles he likes a lot

Burying bones he loves the most
Under trees he hides
Digging in the garden
Dad gets cross
Yippee, he hasn't done it today.

Ella Hayward (6)
Awsworth Primary School, Awsworth

Olivia Fox

Observant
Lively
Imaginative
Valued
Interesting
Amusing

Funky
Open
eXtremely cute.

Olivia Fox (6)
Awsworth Primary School, Awsworth

Dogs

Drink water
Outside to chase cats
Goes and sits on her chair
Shout Molly - my dog.

Megan Paige Eardley (5)
Awsworth Primary School, Awsworth

Fireworks

Fireworks flaring up high,
Inside houses people are warm,
Racing rockets fly about,
Excited people gather around,
Wonderful colours to be seen,
Oh how beautiful they are,
Rosy cheeks under woolly hats,
Keep safe and don't wander,
Snuggle up children, it's time to sleep!

Alice Elphick
Baslow St Anne's CE Primary School, Baslow

Fireworks

Fiery flames passing by.
Indigo fading in the sky,
Racing rockets zooming,
Exploding fireworks booming!
Wonderful colours fill the air.
Open-mouthed people stare.
Roasted marshmallows cooking,
Kiss goodnight.
Stars shining so bright.

Jessica Johnstone Pratt (6)
Baslow St Anne's CE Primary School, Baslow

Fireworks

Fizzy fireworks fill the air,
Indigo flying everywhere,
Red rockets racing,
Excited children chasing,
Wonderful colours,
Oh how exciting,
Roasting sizzling sausages,
Kids playing,
Sparklers sparkling.

Lara Wickersham (6)
Baslow St Anne's CE Primary School, Baslow

Firework

Flaming fireworks fill the air
I love it!
Red rockets race up in the sky
Exploding way up high
Wonderful colours shine
Oliver's eating melting marshmallows
Rosy red cheeks
Keep away from the fire!

Alex Kemp (6)
Baslow St Anne's CE Primary School, Baslow

Bonfire

Burning flames racing through the sky.
On bonfire night it's really scary.
Naughty children playing about near the fire.
Fantastic patterns.
In the fresh darkness.
Rockets launching into the air!
Explode high in the sky.

Harry Goodwin (7)
Baslow St Anne's CE Primary School, Baslow

Bonfire

B ursting cartwheels
O range flames flickering
N oisy children playing games
F izzing sparklers
I am very excited
R osy red cheeks
E xcited children everywhere.

Oliver Kemp (6)
Baslow St Anne's CE Primary School, Baslow

Bonfire

B urning bonfires
O range fiery flames hit the sky,
N oisy children shouting loud.
F lickery flames are beautiful to look at.
I t spreads out like a rainbow.
R ed racing rockets fill the air,
E veryone loves to see the fireworks.

Stephanie Stankard (6)
Baslow St Anne's CE Primary School, Baslow

About Me

K ite flying mad.
A ngry red head.
T errific, brilliant me.
Y oung school child.

Katy Middleton (6)
Belmont Primary School, Swadlincote

All About My Food

Chicken is nice
Ham is pink
Ice cream is nice and cold
Pear is green and juicy
Soup is very warm

At the shops I buy sweets
Nana makes nice cakes
Dinner time

Banana is yellow
Easter eggs
Apple pie and cream
Nougat is chewy
Sausages and spaghetti hoops.

Tegan Harrison (6)
Belmont Primary School, Swadlincote

Animals - Butterfly

Bees buzz
Underground
Tiny ants crawl
Tigers charge
Elephant's trumpet
Rhino's snort
Fish swim
Lions roar
You think of some too!

Millicent Payne (6)
Belmont Primary School, Swadlincote

Emma Thompson In The Park

Everyone was in the park
Meeting all their friends
Mum was watching the kids play
As they chased each other.

They climbed to the top of the climbing frame
'Hello!' they shouted to Mum
'Oh be careful,' said Mum
Monkeying around they raced back down
'Picnic time,' said Mum
Sandwiches, crisps and grapes for all
Off we go, time for bed
Night night Mummy.

Emma Thompson (6)
Belmont Primary School, Swadlincote

Keely Stone

Keely is kind
Everyone likes to play with me
Everyone knows my name
Love is my favourite word
Yoghurt is my second favourite food.

Some people know what I am good at
Television is cool
On my plate I like to eat salmon
Nicole is my sister
Everton is the best football team ever.

Keely Stone (6)
Belmont Primary School, Swadlincote

All about me!

C heeky
A ll he thinks about is karate
M onkey
E ats lots of sweets
R emember his manners
O n Wednesday he goes swimming
N ice.

B ounces on the trampoline
A wesome
T eases the cat called Molly-Moo
E xercises
S ings songs.

Cameron Bates (6)
Belmont Primary School, Swadlincote

Ellie Abley

E llie is 6 years old.
L ikes to feed the fish.
L ovely fish live in the pond.
I have one big fish called Anthony.
E very day I go to school.

A ll the children come out to play.
B oth of my friends like me.
L auren is one of my best friends.
E very day she plays with me.
Y oghurts are my favourite pudding.

Ellie Abley (6)
Belmont Primary School, Swadlincote

Tom And Jerry

Tom is my cat.
Only one year old.
Messy eater.

Always in trouble.
Never does what he is told
Dangles from the curtains.

Jerry is Tom's brother
Ever so shy.
Racing round the garden.
Really soft fur.
Yesterday he did not come home.

Karli Gardner (6)
Belmont Primary School, Swadlincote

Luke Carney

Likes cars.
Under the bed I have cars.
Kid runs around.
Early to bed.

Cars are best.
And planes.
Round and round.
November fireworks.
Eggs for breakfast.
Yawn time for bed.

Luke Carney (6)
Belmont Primary School, Swadlincote

My Family

Joyful
Ambitious
Kind
Exciting
Supper

Fun
Awesome
Mad
Intelligent
Loud
Young.

Jake Noble (7)
Belmont Primary School, Swadlincote

Teddy Bears

Tremendous
Ending
Dream
Doodle
Yes

Breaking heart
Extremely excellent
And cuddly
Really excellent
Super.

Rosie Skidmore (6)
Belmont Primary School, Swadlincote

Jake Simper

J ake is my name
A nd I think it's rather plain
K ieron is in the middle
E veryone thinks it's a fiddle.

S o next comes Simper
I 'm having a little whimper
M um said, 'Stop that noise.'
P lease go and play with your toys
E nter if you dare
R ed paint everywhere!

Jake Simper (6)
Belmont Primary School, Swadlincote

Dogs Rule

D ogs like to play.
O ver the fields they run.
G oing to fetch a ball.
S o they can give it to me.

R unning fast.
U p the hill.
L ovely dogs.
E very dog is great.

Alyssa Watson (7)
Belmont Primary School, Swadlincote

Holidays

Happy and smiling all the time
Outside is where I like to play
Lollies are delicious on the beach
I like to dive into the pool
Dancing is what we do at night
At the fair is my favourite place to be
Yellow sand is by the sea
Spain is a super place to go.

Dione Wildsmith (6)
Belmont Primary School, Swadlincote

Goldfish

Gold swimming
Over and over
Living happy
Dive under
Funny fish
In a bowl
Swimming deep
Happy fish.

Charlotte Robey (6)
Belmont Primary School, Swadlincote

My Cat Lola

Lovely purring cat
Olivia's best friend
Lying on the chair
Always running everywhere

Climbing cat with a spotty back
A beautiful cat
Tail, swishy, wavy.

Olivia Fennell (6)
Belmont Primary School, Swadlincote

My Family

My family love me
Yellow is my mum's favourite colour

Friendly
Ant is my dad's name
My dog is called Rocco
I love my family
Yes I love them.

Taylor Mai McArdle (6)
Belmont Primary School, Swadlincote

Ben

Bright
Energetic
Nice.

Ben Clark (6)
Belmont Primary School, Swadlincote

My Brother

Super
Perfect
Excellent
Cute
Intelligent
Awesome
Lovely.

Jack Cresswell (6)
Belmont Primary School, Swadlincote

The Seaside

Sparkly water
Enormous fishing boats
Angry seagulls
Sandy beach
Ice cream van
Dad's Speedos
Everyone's having fun.

Macey Smith (6)
Belmont Primary School, Swadlincote

Rory

Rory likes playing
Over the fence he goes
Riding on his bike
Yelling at the crows.

Rory Cunningham (6)
Belmont Primary School, Swadlincote

Cookie

Cleaning and tidying
Opening drawers, putting toys away
Oh it's hard work
Keeping my room clean
I try hard
Each time I get a star.

Cameron Cook (6)
Belmont Primary School, Swadlincote

Maisie

Maisie is my name.
A,b, c is as easy as 1, 2, 3.
I am kind to people.
School is fun,
I have a brother called Noah.
Egg and soldier is my favourite.

Maisie Gwilliam (6)
Belmont Primary School, Swadlincote

Winter

Wet and windy
It is ice-cold
Nice and warm in the house
The snow is now falling outside
Everywhere is white
Ready to go sledging.

Jemma Watson (6)
Belmont Primary School, Swadlincote

Me

Lauren is my name.
All I do is play.
Use a torch at night
Reading is fun.
Eat fishfingers and pizza.
Night light helps me sleep.

Lauren Edden (6)
Belmont Primary School, Swadlincote

School

Spelling
Counting
Happy
Optimistic
Opportunity
Learn.

George Pritchard (6)
Belmont Primary School, Swadlincote

All About Me

Jakob is my name
All day long I play
Kicking a ball, riding my bike
On a lovely sunny day
Being with my friend is fun.

Jakob Lachs (6)
Belmont Primary School, Swadlincote

My Football

Wells is my last name.
Excellent football is my game.
Long legs for running fast.
Long arms for big throw-ins.
Saving goals is what I do best.

Ben Wells (7)
Belmont Primary School, Swadlincote

Happy Horse

Horses make me happy.
And frogs do too.
Ponies are smaller.
People ride horses.
You can too.

Molly Gould (6)
Belmont Primary School, Swadlincote

Raindrops

R ain is fun and jumping is fun too.
A nd wellies for jumping definitely are included.
I n golden rain of raindrops.
N ot very nice because you can't play out.
D iamond raindrops sparkle at night.
R ain falls from the sky and makes you wet.
O h dear I have got wet.
P uddles make you wet.
S plash! Splash! Splash! Splash! Splash! Splash!

Cassie Rickwood (6)
Blackwell Primary School, Blackwell

Raindrops

R ain is fun
A mazing shiny raindrops
I n the golden rain
N eed my new shiny wellies
D iamond raindrops
R eally wet
O n my head
P ouring down from the sky
S ky-diving from the clouds.

Erin Miles (6)
Blackwell Primary School, Blackwell

Raindrops

R ain is fun
A wonderful shiny raindrop
I n the golden rain
N eed my new shiny wellies
D iamond raindrops sparkle
R ainbow is up in the sky
O utside the puddles growing
P uddles are dirty
S lippery puddles are funny.

Ella Clarke (6)
Blackwell Primary School, Blackwell

Raindrops

R ain leaves muddy puddles.
A nd you need a raincoat when it rains.
I n rain you can slip.
N o one likes rain.
D d people go out in the rain?
R ain is so, so, so wet when you go out.
O utside puddles are growing.
P uddles are muddy and wet.
S ome puddles are fun to jump in.

Riley Ball (7)
Blackwell Primary School, Blackwell

Raindrops

R ain is fun
A wonderful shiny raindrop.
I n the golden rain.
N eed my new shiny wellies.
D iamond raindrops sparkle.
R ain and sun make a rainbow.
O n my coat peg.
P eople are playing in the rain.
S plash, splash, splash.

Nathan Owens (6)
Blackwell Primary School, Blackwell

Raindrops

R aindrops are fun to play in.
A puddle is big and little sometimes.
I n the rain it's fun for playing.
N eed a hood for the rain for you.
D rops on your head.
R ain drops are fun to look at.
O n the windows you can see rain.
P op on your coat.
S ometimes it rains.

Fabien Oud (6)
Blackwell Primary School, Blackwell

Raindrops

R ain is fun to play in
A wonderful rainy day
I n the rain it makes noise
N eed wellies in rain
D iamond rain is beautiful
R ain makes muddy puddles
O n the ground
P uddles are fun to jump in
S parkly raindrops are fun to watch falling down.

Taylor Wortley (6)
Blackwell Primary School, Blackwell

Raindrops

R ain is fun
A nd rain and sun make a rainbow
I n the rain it is cold
N eed an umbrella because it is wet
D aisy likes splashing in puddles
R ain sparkles
O range juice is as wet as rain
P uddles are messy
S lippery puddles are funny.

Daisy Jakymelen (7)
Blackwell Primary School, Blackwell

Raindrops

R aincoat
A n umbrella
I s wet
N ot irresistible for me
D rip-drop
R eally fun
O range flowers like rain
P uddles
S lips.

Madeleine Childs (6)
Blackwell Primary School, Blackwell

Raindrops

R ain is fun
A wonderful raindrop
I s falling on my head
N eed my umbrella
D on't get wet
R aindrops are wet
O h my teddy is wet
P lop! Look it is a puddle
S plash, splish, splosh.

Jade Taylor (7)
Blackwell Primary School, Blackwell

Raindrops

Rain is fun because of puddles
And then dry easily
In the sun the puddles dry
Need your coat hood up
Did you know rain can wet you?
Rain is lots of fun
On the funfair rain is fun
Put your hood up
Splash!

Emily Hill (6)
Blackwell Primary School, Blackwell

Raindrops

Rain is fun
A wonderful shiny raindrop
In the golden rain
Need my new shiny wellies
Diamond raindrops sparkle
Really wet coat
On my coat peg
People are playing in the rain
Splash, splash, splash.

Courtney Madderson (6)
Blackwell Primary School, Blackwell

Beach Hut

B rilliant, marvellous
E njoyable fun
A cross the beach
C ream yum, yum
H appy children

H ungry people
U nder the cliffs
T hat was fun.

James Walker (6)
Brooklands Primary School, Long Eaton

Starfish

S hining shells
T wisting in the rock pools
A ll in the sand
R ound the rock pool
F ish swimming in the sea
I nside the sea
S andy shells
H ats in the air.

Amy Woollard (6)
Brooklands Primary School, Long Eaton

Starfish

Sea
Twisting seaweed,
Around the rock pool,
Riding rock,
Fish swimming in the sea,
Inside a rock pool,
Shimmery shells,
High cliffs.

Grace Leatherland (6)
Brooklands Primary School, Long Eaton

Dolphin

Dolphins jump up and down
On a motor scooter
Like a bird with lovely fins
Probably I would like to play too
Helping friends if they're deaf
I can ride on a dolphin
Nice dolphins.

Teigan Smith (6)
Brooklands Primary School, Long Eaton

Holiday

H ot holiday, they are hot, hot.
O h the best holiday ever.
L onely in the morning.
I t's good to be on holiday, good, really good.
D anger and traffic on Saturdays.
A nd donkeys ride with people on their back.
Y ippee! I love holidays.

Ryan Kidsley (6)
Brooklands Primary School, Long Eaton

Holiday

H ot holiday is hot, hot, hot.
O ctopus was swimming in the sea.
L obster was on the sand.
I saw a stingray in the water.
D onkey was happy.
A rock was freezing.
Y ummy, scrummy picnic.

Kerina Anup (6)
Brooklands Primary School, Long Eaton

Sand

S and is soft
A nd sprinkly
N udging water
D ay has gone.

Millie Bennett (6)
Brooklands Primary School, Long Eaton

Dolphin

Dolphin dives down deep
Outside and inside, on the seashore
Lovely creatures like to play with balls in the sea
Probably like an arcade
Helping people and friends
I ride on his back every day
Never nudge him or he will get angry.

Siân Devlin (7)
Brooklands Primary School, Long Eaton

Seabed

Sea
Eating fish
Always sharks eating
Back always silky
Electric eels
Down in the sea.

Tyler Marshall (7)
Brooklands Primary School, Long Eaton

Ships

Smashing all around.
Heading to the shore.
In the deep sea.
Port at the shore.
Stopping at the bay.

Harvey Marriott (6)
Brooklands Primary School, Long Eaton

Crabs

C rawls across the sand.
R unning to my feet.
A nd biting them.
B ig crab steps next to the rocks.
S ome crabs chase off other crabs.

Marley Fearon (6)
Brooklands Primary School, Long Eaton

Ice cream

I like ice cream
C ones are soft
E yore! I am on a donkey

C limb a wave
R un for your life
E yore! I got a donkey
A big hole that we have dug
M e and my mummy and my daddy love ice cream!

Tilly Hardy (6)
Christ Church CE Primary School, Chesterfield

Shark

S harks are dangerous
H e can swim fast
A shark can smell blood, they're
R eally naughty when they smell food
K ing sharks eat lots of people.

Tyler Martin (6)
Christ Church CE Primary School, Chesterfield

Dolphins

Dolphins beat their tales
Old dolphins are great
Large fins
Penguins are humungous
Hermit crabs
Insects
Nose is big and grey.

Calum Robertson (6)
Christ Church CE Primary School, Chesterfield

Sharks

Sometimes sharks can be very strict with people
Have small eyes and can see well
Able to whip their tale to help them
Really energetic
King sharks like the taste of blood
Sleep good.

Elena Hancock (7)
Christ Church CE Primary School, Chesterfield

Shark

Sharp teeth and swims in the beautiful sea
Handsome, has got no hands
Are very dangerous and scary
Really quiet so they can sneak up on you
Kills people so be careful.

Grace Lomas (6)
Christ Church CE Primary School, Chesterfield

Shells

Splashing fish in the sea
Hard crab shells
Everyone collects shells
Lovely smooth shells
Long boat ride
Sometimes you find starfish.

Eden Bradbury (6)
Christ Church CE Primary School, Chesterfield

Shark

S scary and white
Horrible blue eyes
A shark is really scary
Raw people would be nice!
Knows where to get food.

Liam Jackson (6)
Christ Church CE Primary School, Chesterfield

Shark

Scarlett was scared because she saw a shark
Hides at the bottom of the sea
A shark has pointy shiny teeth
Really quiet so they can sneak up on you
Korben went to the sea and saw a shark.

Ayiana Denwood (6)
Christ Church CE Primary School, Chesterfield

Shark

Sharks are very good at swimming with their fins.
He is very good at eating bad people.
A shark has shiny white pointed sharp teeth.
Really fast swimmer.
Kills very naughty people.

Ben Clarke (6)
Christ Church CE Primary School, Chesterfield

Shark

Sharks have seven fins
Handsome and glide smoothly through the water
A tail frantically moves him around swishing him around
Really dangerous when hungry
Kills people and likes blood!

Korben Walker (7)
Christ Church CE Primary School, Chesterfield

Crab

Crabs have very sharp claws
Red crabs like to go in the water
A lobster came and ate the crab
Buries himself in the sand.

Jacob King (6)
Christ Church CE Primary School, Chesterfield

Sea

Splash on the beach
Everyone enjoys swimming in the sea
Always freezing cold.

Anisha Nazeem (6)
Christ Church CE Primary School, Chesterfield

Emma Rose Barker

Excellent
Marvellous
Magical
Amazing

Responsible
Outstanding
Sensible
Explorer

Barbie lookalike
Athletic
Reliable
Kind
Extremely nice
Really lovely.

Emma Barker (6)
Fairfield Primary School, Stapleford

Elias Serghi

E xcellent
L ovely
I mportant
A mazing
S uper

S illy
E xhausted
R acer
G reat
H andsome
I nteresting.

Elias Serghi (6)
Fairfield Primary School, Stapleford

All About Me

A mazing
M arvellous
I ncredible
E xcellent

T errific
A great friend
Y ou would love me
L ovely
O utstanding
R eliable.

Amie Taylor (6)
Fairfield Primary School, Stapleford

Lola Mooney

Lovely
Outstanding
Listens well
Amazing

Magical
Over the top
Over dramatic
Nice
Exciting
You just want to meet me!

Lola Mooney (7)
Fairfield Primary School, Stapleford

My Name Is Jessica

Jolly joke
Exciting
Super
Surfer
Incredible
Caring
Amazing.

Jessica Haresign (6)
Fairfield Primary School, Stapleford

Hannah

H appy
A mazing
N ever naughty
N ice
A princess
H andsome.

Hannah Dickinson (5)
Fairfield Primary School, Stapleford

Sophie

S uper
O utstanding
P retty
H elpful
I ncredible
E ager.

Sophie Wheeler (6)
Fairfield Primary School, Stapleford

Martin

M agic
A mazing
R abbit lover
T errific
I nteresting
N ice.

Martin Valtchanov (5)
Fairfield Primary School, Stapleford

Aaron

Amazing
A good boy
Ready
Outstanding
Nice.

Aaron Percival (6)
Fairfield Primary School, Stapleford

Amy

Adorable
Marvellous
Yummy.

Amy Percival (5)
Fairfield Primary School, Stapleford

Katie Leigh

Kind to people
And always helpful
Tomatoes are my favourite
I am good
Everybody is my friend

Lovely long hair
Enjoy school
I love school
Great class
Helpful and happy.

Katie-Leigh (7)
Highwood Player Infant School, Bilborough

Amberleigh

Always smiling
My hair is short and brown and shiny
Being kind to children
Every day I play outside
Rabbits are my favourite
Like riding my bike
Everyone is my friend
I love school
Great at singing
Happy smiling face.

Amberleigh Hancox (6)
Highwood Player Infant School, Bilborough

Katarzyna

Kind every single day
Animals are my favourite thing of all
Talking to nice people
Apples are my favourite fruit
Rowing is good for me
Zip on my coat
Y you can see me in school
Never nasty
Active all of the time.

Katarzyna Kil (7)
Highwood Player Infant School, Bilborough

Courtney

C ats like me
O n the go
U p goes my balloon
R eally I am good
T eatime for me
N ice to people
E verybody looks after me
Y ellow is the colour of my school T-shirt.

Courtney Rowland (6)
Highwood Player Infant School, Bilborough

McKenzie

M y hair is short
C ars are my favourite thing
K ind to people
E very day I play outside
N ice
Z ip on my clothes
I am tall
E verybody likes me.

McKenzie Savage (6)
Highwood Player Infant School, Bilborough

Maddison

M ad
A dorable
D ancing
D ippy
I nteresting
S mart
O nly one
N ice.

Maddison Larcombe (6)
Highwood Player Infant School, Bilborough

Lavelle

L ead a dog
A mazing
V ery sporty
E yes full
L azy
L ovely
E xcited.

Lavelle Bennet (6)
Highwood Player Infant School, Bilborough

Kye

K ind to my friends
Y ou can see me on my hummer bike
E very day I go to school.

Kye Thompson (6)
Highwood Player Infant School, Bilborough

Shekera

S is for share
H is for happy
E is for energy
K is for Kaitain, she's my friend
E is for Elias, he tells me jokes
R is for reading
A is for apple, they are healthy for you.

Shekera Francis (6)
Highwood Player Infant School, Bilborough

Shania

S is for smile
H is for happy
A is for active
N is for nicely
I is for ice cream
A is for acting.

Shania Clark
Highwood Player Infant School, Bilborough

Paige

Pretty, long, blonde, wavy hair
Always a gorgeous smile
I am always nice and good
Great at reading very hard school books
Every day I am very good at lining up.

Paige Bamford (6)
Highwood Player Infant School, Bilborough

Meghan

M arvellous girl
E xciting
G o! Go! Go!
H appy home
A dorable
N ice person.

Meghan Spencer-Sanders (6)
Highwood Player Infant School, Bilborough

Jaydan

J oy
A ction man
Y oung
D ance
A lways chatting
N osy.

Jaydan Walker (6)
Highwood Player Infant School, Bilborough

Samuel

S uper
A ction
M arvellous
U p with coolness
E xperimental
L ovely person.

Samuel Davis (6)
Highwood Player Infant School, Bilborough

Taylor

Talk too much
Always being kind to my friends
You can see me on my bike
Love splashing in puddles
On my trampoline I can bounce high
Running fast around my garden with my black dog.

Taylor Wheeldon (6)
Highwood Player Infant School, Bilborough

Kieron

Kicking
Incredible
Eyes
Run
On
Nice.

Kieron McCarty (6)
Highwood Player Infant School, Bilborough

Taniya

Time for dinner Taniya
Angry sometimes
Nice time
I can play with my friends
Yes I love my mummy
Amazing.

Taniya Baptiste (6)
Highwood Player Infant School, Bilborough

Niamh

N ever naughty
I 'm healthy
A ll I am is good
M y hair is at the side
H ello my name is Niamh.

Niamh Sturdy (6)
Highwood Player Infant School, Bilborough

Carla

C ats are furry and cute
A lways happy
R ed sparkly shoes to match my party dress
L ove eating healthy food
A lways doing hard work.

Carla De Silva (6)
Highwood Player Infant School, Bilborough

Corey

C is for clever
O is for outrageous
R is for really good artist
E is for eating
Y is for yummy.

Corey Staniforth (6)
Highwood Player Infant School, Bilborough

Reece

R abbits are cutest animals
E ating healthy food and vegetables
E verybody is kind to me
C hocolate cakes are my favourite
E lias is my friend.

Reece Howitt (6)
Highwood Player Infant School, Bilborough

Elias

E is for excellent work
L is for lovely work
I is for interesting work
A is for amazing work
S is for smart work.

Elias White (6)
Highwood Player Infant School, Bilborough

Katie

K is for Katie
A is for active
T is for tennis
I is for injury
E is for empty.

Katie Wilson (6)
Highwood Player Infant School, Bilborough

Chris

Charming and smart
Handsome
Rocket
Incredible
Super!

Christopher Marriot (6)
Highwood Player Infant School, Bilborough

Scott

Sometimes my tooth comes out
Cleaning
Open
Teeth
Time.

Scott Kirkham (6)
Highwood Player Infant School, Bilborough

Ellie

Exciting girl
Lovely person
Likeable
Intelligent face
Ellie.

Ellie Goldhawk (6)
Highwood Player Infant School, Bilborough

Megan

Marvellous toys
Expert at writing
Goes on a bike
Aged 7
Nice ride.

Megan Benner (7)
Highwood Player Infant School, Bilborough

Katie

Kind girl
Adorable
Tiny
Interesting
Excellent.

Katie Mullins (6)
Highwood Player Infant School, Bilborough

Tyler

Treasure my mum
Yellow blanket
Lead the dog
Eat McDonald's
Read hard books and chapter books.

Tyler Sturdy (6)
Highwood Player Infant School, Bilborough

Neeco

N oisy
E ntertaining
E nergetic
C uddly
O nly one!

Neeco Wallace (6)
Highwood Player Infant School, Bilborough

Ryan

R ed blanket
Y ellow yoyo
A mazing
N oisy Ryan!

Ryan Tuckwood (6)
Highwood Player Infant School, Bilborough

Kain

K is for kindness
A is for adding
I is for interesting
N is for nice.

Kain Fletcher (6)
Highwood Player Infant School, Bilborough

Tia

Tiny
Interesting
Adorable.

Tia Parker (6)
Highwood Player Infant School, Bilborough

Tia

T is for talking
I is for interesting
A is for amazing.

Tia Rhodes (6)
Highwood Player Infant School, Bilborough

J-Lo

Jumpy fun
Loveable rogue
Octopus.

J-Lo Ayres (6)
Highwood Player Infant School, Bilborough

Myself

Today I am happy
Yesterday I was sad
Like drawing and
Eating cake
Really happy.

Tyler Hill (6)
Lake View Primary & Nursery School, Rainworth

Myself

C hatty
H am sandwiches are my favourite
A nd
R ed is my favourite colour
L ove to sleep
O n my sofa
T ortoises are my favourite animal
T iny
E ntertaining.

Charlotte Reynolds (6)
Lake View Primary & Nursery School, Rainworth

Rebecca

R ed is my favourite colour
E nergetic
B rave
E xciting
C aring
C ats are my second favourite animal
A lways like cake.

Rebecca Norris (6)
Lake View Primary & Nursery School, Rainworth

Myself

'Ginger the Stray Kitten' is my favourite book
Energetic
Orange is my third favourite colour
Ready for anything
Ginger biscuits are my favourite snack
Ice skating is good
Always happy.

Georgia Hind (7)
Lake View Primary & Nursery School, Rainworth

Myself

Clever
Always happy
Interesting
Toast is my favourite
Lovely
I like my mummy
Number work is my favourite.

Caitlin Stendall (6)
Lake View Primary & Nursery School, Rainworth

Myself

Jam on toast is my favourite
Always happy
Doesn't like ham
Energetic.

Jade Samuels (6)
Lake View Primary & Nursery School, Rainworth

Myself

Makes people happy
I like eating jam tarts
Cool
Helpful
Always smiling
Everlasting jumpers
Like lions.

Michael Keam (6)
Lake View Primary & Nursery School, Rainworth

Myself

My favourite colour is black
Always good
Talking to my mummy
Tall
Happy
Eating chips
With red sauce.

Matthew Eastwood (6)
Lake View Primary & Nursery School, Rainworth

Myself

My favourite toy is a dog and
Yellow is its colour
Always kind.

Mya Barker (6)
Lake View Primary & Nursery School, Rainworth

Myself

M odest and magic
I like my trains
C aring
H elpful
A lways helpful and truthful
E nergetic
L ate is something I don't like to be.

Michael Anderson (6)
Lake View Primary & Nursery School, Rainworth

Myself

A lways happy
B ig
I like pink
G ames are my favourite thing
A sleep is good for you
I like games
L ike ice skating.

Abigail Pearson (6)
Lake View Primary & Nursery School, Rainworth

Myself

C aring
H appy
E nergetic
L ike my mum because she hugs me
S easide is my favourite place
E ating cake is the best
A lways smiling.

Chelsea Parry (6)
Lake View Primary & Nursery School, Rainworth

Myself

M y favourite colour is blue
O ranges are my favourite fruit
R abbits are my favourite animal
G iggly
A lways chatty
N ever sad.

Morgan Harrison (6)
Lake View Primary & Nursery School, Rainworth

Myself

C lever
H appy
L ike to run around in the playground
O range is my second favourite colour
E xcited.

Chloe Moore (7)
Lake View Primary & Nursery School, Rainworth

Myself

Energetic
Like playing with my toys
Love my sister
I like playing on my trampoline
Eggs are my favourite food.

Ellie Middlebrook (7)
Lake View Primary & Nursery School, Rainworth

Myself

Happy all the time
Orange is my third favourite colour
Like to do ice skating
Love my sister
Yesterday I did some maths.

Holly Rodgers (7)
Lake View Primary & Nursery School, Rainworth

Myself

Always happy
I like my toys
Dogs are my friends
Energetic
Never sad.

Aiden Hutchison (6)
Lake View Primary & Nursery School, Rainworth

Myself

Really happy and likes
Eating chips and
Eggs
Chatty
Energetic.

Reece Daines (6)
Lake View Primary & Nursery School, Rainworth

Myself

Eggs are my favourite
Teachers are my favourite
Holidays are the best
All my friends are nice
Never cry.

Ethan Warnes (6)
Lake View Primary & Nursery School, Rainworth

Myself

My favourite colour is pink
Always smiling
Reading books is my favourite thing
Nice
Yak is my favourite animal.

Marny Persaud (6)
Lake View Primary & Nursery School, Rainworth

Myself

J am sandwiches
A nts are my favourite insects
M y favourite colour is red
I like my cars
E ggs on toast are Grandad's favourite.

Jamie Salter (7)
Lake View Primary & Nursery School, Rainworth

Amazing Benjamin

B rilliantly always helpful
E xcited supporting Manchester United
N aughty at work
J olly playing football
A mazing in school
M agical in maths
I nventive in making models
N asty to girls!

Benjamin Butler (7)
Longford Parochial CE Primary School, Ashbourne

Emily

E xcited
M agical
I nteresting
L ittle and lovely
Y ou will like me.

Emily Sessions (5)
Longford Parochial CE Primary School, Ashbourne

Autumn

Amazing leaves spinning down
Unusual colours on the trees
Twirly leaves falling to the ground
Under the burrow a rabbit lies
Magnificent colours float around hiding
Nutty treats for the squirrels.

Lydia Hunter (6)
Longford Parochial CE Primary School, Ashbourne

Autumn

Amazing wind blowing the leaves
Unusual colours of the leaves
Twirly leaves falling off the trees
Unbelievably hard conkers crashing to the ground
Massive conkers breaking in fights
Nights are getting longer when the foxes come out.

Evan Hope (7)
Longford Parochial CE Primary School, Ashbourne

Joshua

Jump out of bed
Or on my trampoline
Sensible at school
Hopping on one leg
Unusual at swimming
Amazing boy!

Joshua Phillips (5)
Longford Parochial CE Primary School, Ashbourne

Toby

T rouble to my brothers
O r my mum and dad
B ossy me
Y oungest in my family.

Toby Ainsworth (6)
Longford Parochial CE Primary School, Ashbourne

All About Ben

B ig and bouncy Ben
E xcited all the time
N ice to my friends and family.

Benjamin Lewis (5)
Longford Parochial CE Primary School, Ashbourne

Pirates

P olly the parrot
I s sat on the pirate's shoulder
R ings are shiny in the box
A nchor goes deep in the ocean
T he treasure is lost
E verything is spooky
S torms are on the way.

Effie Sugden (6)
Lovers' Lane Primary School, Newark-on-Trent

Pirates

P arrot talks to the pirate
I see an incredible island
R oger flies really high in the sky
A nchor gets lowered down to the sea
T ops are all ragged
E vil pirates are up ahead
S ea gets really wild - ooh heck!

Abby Louise Brown (6)
Lovers' Lane Primary School, Newark-on-Trent

Pirates

P irates are lost in the ship
I sland ahead
R oger flag flies in the air
A parrot says 'Island ahead.'
T reasure glows in the sky
E xplorers investigate on the island
S ails blow in the wind.

Cody Wainwright-Lees (6)
Lovers' Lane Primary School, Newark-on-Trent

Pirates

P irates snooze on the ship
I sland above
R oger flying in the air
A nchor in the sea
T reasure is shiny
E xcited pirates
S hout, 'Hooray, hooray, hooray!'

Josh Hope (6)
Lovers' Lane Primary School, Newark-on-Trent

Pirates

'P irates is that an island over there?'
'I think it is.'
'R opes pull,' they say
A nchor thrown it to stop the ship
'T ea, get my tea!'
E ven now we are not safe
'S ea monster! Quick go!'

Jaxon Fixter (6)
Lovers' Lane Primary School, Newark-on-Trent

Pirates

Pirates walk the plank
I'm scared
Rings are on my fingers
Adventure awaits
Trousers are ripped
Eating chips
Shiny sword.

Paige Hubbard (6)
Lovers' Lane Primary School, Newark-on-Trent

Pirates

Pirate ship is brown and mouldy
It is dark and stinky too
Rope is up and dusty
A rat came in and bit my toe
Teeth are dirty
Evil men coming 'Get your sword'
Sea monster coming!

Byron Rees Watson (6)
Lovers' Lane Primary School, Newark-on-Trent

Pirates

Pirate ship sail on the high seas
'Island ahead' said the parrot
Rest your sleepy head
Anchor stops the boat
Treasure ahead
Excited pirates dancing
Shouting and singing too.

Chloe Morrison (6)
Lovers' Lane Primary School, Newark-on-Trent

Pirates

Pirates set sail on an adventure
I can see an island in front of me
Right let's have a party
Apple to munch
Time to fire the cannons
Egg for lunch
Snoozing in the night.

Emily Hibberd (6)
Lovers' Lane Primary School, Newark-on-Trent

Pirates

Pirate Polly Parrot
Island is up ahead
Roger red water
Adventure time is here
Treasure up ahead
Excited pirate men
Swords clatter clack.

Charlie Lee (6)
Lovers' Lane Primary School, Newark-on-Trent

Pirates

Pirates' ship sailed quietly
In we go into the dark cave
Roger swooping in the air
Anchor thrown in the sea
Tip the boat
Easy, get the boat back
Splashing the water.

Seth Young (6)
Lovers' Lane Primary School, Newark-on-Trent

Farmwork

H elping on the farm
A round all the fields
R iding on tractors
V ery good fun
E arly morning jobs
S unny and bright
T ime for tea, done for the night.

Carl Green (5)
Lovers' Lane Primary School, Newark-on-Trent

The Happy Harvest

H arvest time is once a year
A rrival of wheat fills the farmer with cheer
R eady with his combine harvester
V ery happy that God has been so kind this year
E very crop so precious and dear
S o there is plenty of food to share
T ime to say goodbye, until the next harvest time.

Vlad Troshkov (5)
Lovers' Lane Primary School, Newark-on-Trent

Harvest Time

Harvest time is here again
Autumn is upon us
Reaping and gathering
Vegetables and fruit
Every farmer is celebrating
Success of their crops
Thanksgiving for the harvest.

Shannon Cowdell (5)
Lovers' Lane Primary School, Newark-on-Trent

Food

Hay
Animals' winter food
Ripened wheat
Vast fields
Ears used to make bread
Sugar beet too
Taken to make sugar.

George Silver (6)
Lovers' Lane Primary School, Newark-on-Trent

Harvest

H arvest is a lovely time
A pples falling off the trees
R abbits are hoping and playing
V egetables are ready to eat
E veryone feels it is a lovely time
S un is shining
T rees have grown.

Jessica McDowall (5)
Lovers' Lane Primary School, Newark-on-Trent

Apples

H eaps of
A pples
R ed, red apples
V ery, very juicy
E verybody eats
S weet, sweet apples
T asty, tasty red apples.

Lewis Walker (5)
Lovers' Lane Primary School, Newark-on-Trent

The Love Of The Land

H ooray it's that time of year again
A ll got our wellies to be out in the rain
R emembering it's our harvest festival trip
V aluing each other, we give tins for the sick
E erybody joins in with helping hands
S inging the songs along with the band
T he love has been spread all over the land.

Bradley Fletcher (6)
Lovers' Lane Primary School, Newark-on-Trent

Harvest

H arvest is a happy time
A pples and fruit come
R abbits come out to play
V iolins are musical
E ating is very special
S ummer has ended
T rees are changing.

Noah Potter (5)
Lovers' Lane Primary School, Newark-on-Trent

Cats

C reepy
A nimals
T apping on the window ledge
S itting down.

Chloe Weatherilt (5)
Newtown Primary School, New Mills

Basketball

B alls
A re tall
S pace
K eep the score
E xercise
T hrow it
B ounce
A im at the net
L ong legs
L ots of fun.

Jacob Hill (6)
Newtown Primary School, New Mills

Thunder

T hunder and lightning
H ere it comes!
U mbrella
N oise
D ark sky
E xciting
R eally scared.

Abigail Tovey (5)
Newtown Primary School, New Mills

Joshua

Jogging
Orange hair
Sad
Happy
Uniform
Apples.

Joshua Brookes (6)
Newtown Primary School, New Mills

Alarm

A warning!
Lights
Alarm
Replace
Makes a noise.

Jack Currington (6)
Newtown Primary School, New Mills

Books

Books on the bookshelf
One person alone
OK, books
Kind books
Stories are good.

Charlotte Dodd (6)
Newtown Primary School, New Mills

Becky, My Sister

B ossy sister!
E lephant stomps
C rying when she's away
K isses me
Y ummy stuff.

Sophie Allsop (7)
Newtown Primary School, New Mills

Peas

P eas are nice
E at your peas
A re yummy
S lip off the plate.

Thomas Price (6)
Newtown Primary School, New Mills

Playtime

P layground fun
L istening in the playground
A ll alone in the playground is not fun
Y ellow sun shining bright
T om dancing in the playground
I like the playground
M ia sharing in the sun
E lla playing in the playground.

Amber Simms (6)
Ranby CE Primary School, Retford

Playground

Playtime activities
Looking at birds flying in the sky
All excited children
Yelling teachers
Giggling little people, giggling at you
Running big ones, darting past me
Obstacle course
Unfair games, not allowed
Nibbling teachers eating apples
Dan, drinking milk on the bench.

Tom Wendon (7)
Ranby CE Primary School, Retford

Playtime

People shouting funny words
Laughing friends
Amazing people
Yelling everywhere
Tagging and jumping in the sun
I jump in the snow making marks
My brother chasing me
Everybody having lots of fun.

Mia Walters (6)
Ranby CE Primary School, Retford

Playtime

People laugh and run around
Laughing children
Always equipment sharing
Yelling children
Tom darting round
Isobel and Ella running
Munching food
Everyone is friends.

Jacob Gascoyne (7)
Ranby CE Primary School, Retford

Playtime

Playtime having fun giggling
Laughing, playing, with my friends
All our equipment outside in the playground sun
Yelling as loud as you can
Tom yelling to his friends
I can see leaves falling
Millie talking
Emma listening.

Ella Brewer (6)
Ranby CE Primary School, Retford

Playtime

P laytime fun people smiling
L aughing children
A ll the people laughing
Y oung people laughing
T iny people sharing
E njoy the fun
M y friends shouting
E njoy fruit, munch, munch.

Josie Walker (6)
Ranby CE Primary School, Retford

My Space Poem

S un is hot and big
O range can be the sun
L ittle rockets
A stronauts fly
R eally cool space.

S tars are cool
Y ellow is the sun
S aturn has rings
T he sun is bright
E arth is big
M ars is big.

Cameron West-Somacarrera (5)
St Edward's RC Primary School, Swadlincote

Solar System

Stars are hot
Oh the sun is orange and yellow
Listen, life on Mars
Astronauts live in space
Rockets land on the moon.

Sun is hot
You can see the sun
Sun is bright and hot
Titan planets are nice
Earth is different colours
Moon is lovely.

Eleanor Critchlow (5)
St Edward's RC Primary School, Swadlincote

My Space Poem

Space
Pluto
Aliens
Comets
Earth.

Joshua Cotton & Tyler Roberts Drew (5)
St Edward's RC Primary School, Swadlincote

Space Poem

S pace
P luto
A liens
C omets
E arth.

Macie Cooke (5)
St Edward's RC Primary School, Swadlincote

Marshall

M arshall plays with Ben
A ll my friends are fun
R unning to the shop for my dad
S adly my one dog died but one stayed alive
H olidays at Fornnby are fun
A fter school I play out
L azy Marshall sleeps in his sleeping bag
L iam is my brother.

Marshall-Robert Bannister (6)
St Margaret's Catholic Primary School, Gamesley

Chelsea

Chelsea plays with Frankie
Hungry Chelsea likes crisps
Elephants are big and grey
Laughing Chelsea laughs at her dad
See me on my bike
Everybody loves me
All day I like playing with my toys.

Chelsea Tudor (6)
St Margaret's Catholic Primary School, Gamesley

Oliver

Oliver plays football
Long lazy days are great
I love lollipops
Vegetables are tasty
Every day I come to school
Reading is my favourite.

Oliver Woodward (6)
St Margaret's Catholic Primary School, Gamesley

Cailin

Cailin likes birds
A squirrel lives in my garden
I have a best friend next door
Laughing Cailin likes laughing a lot
I have a dog, he is funny
Nana is my babysitter.

Cailin Healey (6)
St Margaret's Catholic Primary School, Gamesley

Kira O'Donnell

Kind
Is a brave star
Runs like the wind
Amazing

Over excited
Dancer
Orange mad
Nice
Nicer than rain
Eats chocolate
Likes gymnastics
Loves singing.

Kira O'Donnell (6)
Walton Holymoorside Primary School, Holymoorside

James Butler

J am
A Lego fan
M usic
E legant
S tories

`B utter
U ltra footballer
T ravis is my brother
L ego Star Wars Saga on the Wii
E legant
R oses.

James Butler (7)
Walton Holymoorside Primary School, Holymoorside

Chloe Hickey

C heeky
H ot
L ovely
O ranges
E xtremely excited.

H appy
I love chocolate
C ool
K icking
E xcited
Y o-yo.

Chloe Hickey (6)
Walton Holymoorside Primary School, Holymoorside

Isaac Morgan

I am intelligent
Smiley boy
A real good friend
An amazing person
Car crazy

Millie is my sister
Oranges are my favourite fruit
Reading is my favourite thing
Great at maths
A fast runner
Nice person.

Isaac Morgan (7)
Walton Holymoorside Primary School, Holymoorside

Ellie Haggar

Excited
Love cats
Love circus
I like colouring
Excited

Holidays
A love of cats
Good at work
Good at looking after friends
A good worker
Running.

Ellie Haggar (6)
Walton Holymoorside Primary School, Holymoorside

Alex Briggs

A music lover
L ettuce
E xcited
X -ray

B lue is my favourite colour
R eally good at running
I like to build
G ood at playing on my DS
G ood at playing on the Wii
S ee beaches.

Alex Briggs (7)
Walton Holymoorside Primary School, Holymoorside

Lucy Payne

L oves chocolate
U nhappy is not funny
C olouring is fun
Y oghurts are nice

P uddings are nice to eat
A pples are lovely
Y o-yos are good
N ice and friendly
E xcited going to parties.

Lucy Payne (6)
Walton Holymoorside Primary School, Holymoorside

Luca Finch

L egs
U p and down on a trampoline
C ounting is brilliant
A lways I wish for salmon.

F ootball is exciting
I ce cream is yummy
N ice fish
C olouring is brilliant
H appy all the time.

Luca Finch (6)
Walton Holymoorside Primary School, Holymoorside

Tom Wood

T ries his best
O range chewing gum
M y favourite game is football.

W icked
O ften plays football
O nly likes playing
D ance with music.

Tom Wood (6)
Walton Holymoorside Primary School, Holymoorside

Alberta

A girl
L olly
B rothers Oscar and Henry
E ating ice cream and popcorn
R ed is my favourite colour
T omato pizza
A mazing at gymnastics.

Alberta Hallam (6)
Walton Holymoorside Primary School, Holymoorside

Rebecca

R eally good at maths
E xcellent at handwriting
B londe curly hair
E ating cake is fantastic
C reative at things
C are for friends
A mazing at swimming.

Rebecca Riley (6)
Walton Holymoorside Primary School, Holymoorside

Aisling

A nice smile
I n the playground
S ometimes looking around
L ovely eyes
I like donuts
N ice gentle hands
G reat fried eggs!

Aisling Woolhouse (6)
Walton Holymoorside Primary School, Holymoorside

Jasmine

J umping girl
A my is my best friend and
S he's wonderful
M arvellous Dad
I 'm a big Michael Jackson fan
N ice girl
E ating sweets is cool.

Jasmine Kerry (7)
Walton Holymoorside Primary School, Holymoorside

Amelia

A girl
M agic maths
E ating strawberries, sweets and popcorn
L ilac
I ce cream
A rms.

Amelia Fletcher (6)
Walton Holymoorside Primary School, Holymoorside

Gemma

G reat at glueing
E nergetic and happy
M akes chocolate cake
M eans well
A friendly girl.

Gemma Hardy (6)
Walton Holymoorside Primary School, Holymoorside

Young Writers Information

We hope you have enjoyed reading this book - and that you will continue to enjoy it in the coming years.

If you like reading and writing poetry drop us a line, or give us a call, and we'll send you a free information pack.

Alternatively if you would like to order further copies of this book or any of our other titles, then please give us a call or log onto our website at www.youngwriters.co.uk.

Young Writers Information
Remus House
Coltsfoot Drive
Peterborough
PE2 9JX
(01733) 890066